CLASS, GENDER, RACE AND COLONIALISM

CLASS, GENDER, RACE & COLONIALISM

THE 'INTERSECTIONALITY' OF MARX

KEVIN B ANDERSON

DARAJA PRESS
&
MONTHLY REVIEW ESSAYS

Published by Daraja Press
https://darajapress.com
in association with
Monthly Review Essays
https://mronline.org/category/monthly-review-essays/

ISBN (soft cover): 978-1-988832-63-0
ISBN ebook: 978-1-988832-64-7

Cover design: Kate McDonnell

Library and Archives Canada Cataloguing in Publication
Title: Class, gender, race & colonialism : the 'intersectionality' of Marx / Kevin B
    Anderson.
Other titles: Class, gender, race and colonialism
Names: Anderson, Kevin, 1948- author.
Description: Series statement: Thinking freedom | "This pamphlet, Class,
    gender, race & colonialism: The 'intersectionality'of Marx, is based on the
    text of the article entitled 'Marx at 200' that was first published by the
    Economic and Political Weekly (Vol.53, Issue No. 40, 06 Oct, 2018) and is
    published here with permission."--Preface. | Includes bibliographical
    references.
Identifiers: Canadiana (print) 20200226738 | Canadiana (ebook) 20200226835 |
    ISBN 9781988832630 (softcover) | ISBN 9781988832647 (ebook)
Subjects: LCSH: Marx, Karl, 1818-1883—Political and social views. | LCSH:
    Humanism—Philosophy.
Classification: LCC JC233.M299 A53 2020 | DDC 335.4—dc23

PUBLISHER'S PREFACE

Marx's writings have sometimes been misrepresented. Many consider them to be no longer relevant for the 21st century on the mistaken assumption that he was obsessed only with class and had little appreciation of how issues of gender, racism and colonialism inter-related with class and the struggle for human emancipation. But as Kevin Anderson explains in this pamphlet:

> It is important to see both [Marx's] brilliant generalisations about capitalist society and the very concrete ways in which he examined not only class, but also gender, race, and colonialism, and what today would be called the intersectionality of all of these. His underlying revolutionary humanism was the enemy of all forms of abstraction that denied the variety and multiplicity of human experience, especially as his vision extended outward from Western Europe. For these reasons, no thinker speaks to us today with such force and clarity.

The pamphlet is part of a series published by *Daraja Press* entitled *Thinking Freedom*. We will be publishing other short, pamphlet-sized publications that address key topics / issues related to current struggles for emancipation, justice, dignity and self-determination targeted at the growing generations of activists, members social movements, and unions. Our aim is to produce short, easy to read, jargon free, pamphlets as print, pdf, ebook and, in some cases, audiobook formats. The pamphlets will aim to stimulate reflection and debate. In some instances, the publications will be accompanied by webinars and podcasts. The idea is to make popular materials that encourage deeper reflection on the meaning and possibilities for emancipatory politics that does not blindly follow established dogma, but reviews the 'classics' and international experiences critically. We have published a series of interviews / podcasts in relation to *Organising in the time of Covid-19* that can be accessed at https://darajapress.com/blog.

If you have suggestions about topics that you think should be included in this series, please get in touch at info[AT]darajapress.com.

Firoze Manji
Publisher, Daraja Press

CLASS, GENDER, RACE & COLONIALISM: THE 'INTERSECTIONALITY' OF MARX

It is clear today that the emancipation of labour from capitalist alienation and exploitation is a task that still confronts us. Marx's concept of the worker is not limited to European white males, but includes Irish and Black super-exploited and therefore doubly revolutionary workers, as well as women of all races and nations. But, his research and his concept of revolution go further, incorporating a wide range of agrarian non-capitalist societies of his time, from India to Russia and from Algeria to the Indigenous peoples of the Americas, often emphasising their gender relations. In his last, still partially unpublished writings, he turns his gaze Eastward and Southward. In these regions outside Western Europe, he finds important revolutionary possibilities among peasants and their ancient communistic social structures, even as these are being undermined by their formal subsumption under the rule of capital. In his last published text, he envisions an alliance between these non-working-class strata and the Western European working class.

1

"Proletarians [*Proletarier*] of all countries, unite!" It is with these ringing words that Karl Marx and Friedrich Engels famously conclude their *Communist Manifesto* in 1848.[1] This suggests a broad class struggle involving millions of workers across national and regional boundaries against their collective enemies, capital and landed property. In that same *Manifesto*, Marx and Engels also write, in another well-known passage, that "the workers have no country," and further that "national differences and antagonisms between peoples [*Völker*] are shrinking more and more" with the development of the capitalist world market.[2]

AN ABSTRACT, GENERAL THEORY OF CAPITAL AND LABOUR

In the *Manifesto*, we are presented with large social forces, the proletariat or working class and its opponents, contending with each other on an international scale, where differences of culture, nationality, and geography have been overturned, or are being overturned, as capital is coming to rule the world and the workers are organising their resistance to it. Marx and Engels are writing here at a very high level of generality, abstracting from the specificities of the life experience of Western European and North American workers, and predicting that their lot will soon become that of the world's working people, at that time mainly peasants labouring in predominantly agrarian societies.

It is in this sense that Marx and Engels also write that capitalism has "through its exploitation of the world market given a cos-

1. MECW 6: 519; MEW 4: 493, sometimes my translation)
2. MECW 6: 502–03; MEW 4: 479

mopolitan character to production and consumption in every country." They add: "National one-sidedness and narrow-mindedness become more and more impossible."[3] Capital creates a world culture alongside its world market, forcing itself into every corner of the globe. They go so far as to applaud, in terms imbued with Eurocentric condescension, how capitalism "draws even the most barbarian nations into civilisation" as it "batters down all Chinese walls" and forces these "barbarians ... to adopt the bourgeois mode of production."[4] While pain is produced as old societies are destroyed, capital is carrying out its historic mission, the creation of "more massive and more colossal productive forces than have all preceding generations put together."[5]

Two decades later, in the 1867 preface to *Capital*, Marx writes, with a similar logic emphasising abstraction, that the "value form" that is at the core of capitalist production cannot be studied only empirically with regard to specific commodities produced. He adds: "Why? Because the complete body is easier to study than its cells." Therefore, to analyse capitalism and its value form properly and fully, one must resort to "the power of abstraction" in order to examine commodity production as a whole.[6]

There is clearly a universalising pull under capitalism, a globalising system whose extension homogenises, regularises, and flattens the world, uprooting and changing it as needed to maximise value production, a quest that forms the soul of a soulless system. That same universalising pull creates a deep contradiction, the revolutionary opposition of the modern working class, "united and

MECW 6: 488
MECW 6: 488
MECW 6: 489
Marx 1976: 90

organised by the very mechanism of the capitalist process of production."[7]

The experience of the working class is similarly homogenised.
Shorn of its means of production (land, tools, etc) and reduced
to a group of propertyless wage labourers, prototypically in giant
factories, Marx's working class is both alienated and exploited in
ways specific to capitalism. As early as 1844 Manuscripts, he wrote
of alienated labour, a concept deepened in Capital in the section of
commodity fetishism. In the capitalist production process, human
relations are fetishised because the products of labour come to
dominate their producers, the workers, in a jarring subject–object
reversal. These workers then experience that domination as the
impersonal power of capital, which is itself produced by their
labour. Capital lords it over them, turning human relations into
"relations between things," with the working class objectified to
the extreme.[8]

Raya Dunayevskaya is among the few to emphasise Marx's addi-
tional statement to the effect that these relations "appear
[erscheinen] as what they are".[9] The German verb erscheinen [like the
word apparaissent he uses at this point in the French edition] is not
a false or "mere" appearance and it differs from scheinen [French:
paraissent], which means "appear" in the sense of semblance or
even false appearance. Thus, we are not dealing with a false appearance that conceals "true" and humanistic human relations, but a
new and unprecedented reality based upon "the necessity of that
appearance because, that is, in truth, what relations among people

7. Marx 1976: 929
8. Marx 1976: 166
9. Marx 1976: 166; MEW 23: 86; Marx 1994: 607

are at the point of production" in a capitalist system.[10] In the long run, of course, such a thing-like human relationship is false in the sense that it will be rejected and uprooted by the working class, which seeks a society controlled not by capital but by free and associated labour. But, it remains utterly real while we are under the sway of the capitalist mode of production.

At the same time, the workers suffer harsh material exploitation, as the surplus value they create in the production process is appropriated by capital, in a system characterised by the greatest gulf in history between the material lot of the dominant classes and those of the working people. This exploitation grows in both absolute and relative terms as capital centralises and develops further technologically, in the process of the greatest quantitative increase in the development of the productive forces in human history.[11]

Marx pulls together these two concepts, exploitation and alienation, in his discussion of capital accumulation, wherein the "capitalist system" turns the labour of the workers into stultifying "torment," serving to "alienate" from the workers "the intellectual potentialities of the labor process," while at the same time, the rate of exploitation increases: "the situation of the worker, be his payment high or low, must grow worse" relative to the vertiginous accumulation of surplus value by capital.[12]

MARX'S CONCRETE DIALECTIC

The kind of analysis presented above shows Marx as our contemporary, not least his grasp of the limitless quest for surplus value

. (Dunayevskaya 1958: 100, emphasis in the original)
. Marx 1976: 929
. Marx 1976: 799

by capital, and the concomitant deep alienation and exploitation that it visits upon the working people, from factories to modern call centres.

At the same time, these kinds of statements, especially when read out of context, have been used for decades by Marx's critics, both conservative and left-wing, to portray him as a thinker whose abstract model of capital and labour occludes national differences, race, ethnicity, gender, and other crucially important aspects of human society and culture.

On the one hand, these critics are wrong because capitalism is in fact a unique social system that overturns and homogenises all previous social relations, tending towards the reduction of all human relations to that of capital versus labour. Thus, one cannot understand contemporary family and gender relations, ethno-racial and communal conflict, or ecological crisis fully without examining the underlying relationships described above. For the family, the ethnic tableau, and the natural environment are all conditioned by the underlying fact of a capitalist mode of production.

But, on the other hand, these critics pose questions that make us look more carefully at Marx's theoretical categories. It is very important in this regard to realise, if one truly wants to appreciate Marx's originality, that his concept of capital and labour was posed not only at a high level of abstraction, but that, at other levels, it encompasses a far wider variety of human experience and culture. As Bertell Ollman[13] has emphasised, Marx operated at varying levels of abstraction.

The present article centres on **three related points**.

- *First*, Marx's working class was not only Western European, white, and male, since from his earliest to his latest writings, he took up the working class in all its human variety.

- *Second*, Marx was not an economic or class reductionist, for throughout his career, he considered deeply various forms of oppression and resistance to capital and the state that were not based entirely upon class, but also upon nationality, race and ethnicity, and gender.

- *Third*, by the time of Marx's later writings, long after the *Communist Manifesto*, the Western European pathway of industrial capitalist development out of feudalism was no longer a global universal. Alternate pathways of development were indeed possible, and these connected to types of revolutions that did not always fit the model of industrial labour overthrowing capital.

In terms of a concrete dialectic, Marx follows in the wake of Georg Wilhelm Friedrich Hegel. This is true from his earliest writings to *Capital*, where he writes of "the Hegelian 'contradiction,' which is the source of all dialectics."[14] One striking feature of Hegel's dialectical framework, despite its overall universalising thrust, is its rejection of abstract universals, while also avoiding a mere empiricism. No previous philosopher had drawn history and social existence into philosophy in this way, as seen especially in the *Phenomenology of Spirit*, a book so crucial to our understanding of the present moment that two new translations of it have appeared in 2018. Again and again in this work, Hegel rejects the abstract universal as "the night in which, as the saying goes, all cows are black."[15]

14. Marx 1976: 744
15. Hegel 2018: 10

The concreteness of his universals is also seen in the ascending concrete forms of consciousness that develop along the universal pathway towards the freedom of the human spirit, from ancient Rome to the Reformation and the French Revolution of his own time, each of them limited by their historical, social, and cultural context. Of course, Marx also rejects aspects of Hegel's idealism, especially his stress on the growth of human consciousness as the most important result of the dialectics of history, as opposed to the actuality of human freedom and healthy development in a society that has been revolutionised from below. In short, Hegel's dialectic, while social and historical, remains somewhat dehumanised.

Such stress on the concrete universal in no way negates my earlier citation, where Marx writes that one needs the "power of abstraction" to get at what is really crucial about capitalism, its value form and the dehumanised, fetishised existence experienced by those who live under its domination. No, the solution has to be approached from both directions. The abstract rests upon the concrete, but at the same time, the abstract concept has to concretise itself, to become determinate. However, Marx equally rejects what Karel Kosík called the "pseudoconcrete," a type of concrete that cannot think beyond the immediately given under capitalism. As against such false or distorted forms of consciousness, dialectics "dissolves fetishised artefacts both of the world of things and the world of ideas, in order to penetrate to their reality."[16]

Thus, Marx is hostile to mere empiricism, embracing a dialectical form of totality. He at the same time castigates, as did Hegel, the abstract universals of traditional idealist philosophy and of modern liberalism, with its human and civil rights that are so often little

16. Kosík 1976: 7

8

more than formulaic to those at the bottom of society. Yet, at the same time, he embraces what he and Hegel called the concrete universal, a form of universality that was rooted in social life, and yet pointed beyond the given world of the "pseudoconcrete."

One example of the concrete universal can be glimpsed in how Marx argues that we cannot adequately measure the world of capitalist exploitation and alienation either in its own terms (the "pseudoconcrete") or by comparing it to past forms of domination like Western European feudalism, the ancient Greco–Roman world, or the "Asiatic" mode of production. Instead, he measures capitalist society against a different yardstick, the unrealised but potentially realisable horizon of a communist future of free and associated labour, as has been emphasised in two recent studies.[17] But, this is not merely an imagined republic, as Niccolò Machiavelli characterised the abstract and schematic models of the good society found in ancient Greco–Roman thinkers like Socrates. Marx's vision of the future was based upon the aspirations and struggles of a really existing social class, the proletariat, to which his writings sought to give a more universal and concrete form.

THE WORKING CLASS IN ALL ITS HUMAN VARIETY

From the outset, Marx saw Britain as the country where the capitalist mode of production was most developed, far ahead of any other country. This can be seen especially in *Capital*, where British examples of both capital and labour predominate. But the British working class was by no means homogenous. As the industrial rev-

Hudis 2012; Chattopadhyay 2016

olution surged in Manchester, the cutting-edge city of 19th-century capitalism, it did so by exploiting a working class with deep ethnic divisions between English and Irish workers. Engels discusses this issue at length in his 1845 book, *The Condition of the Working Class in England* published just after he and Marx began to collaborate. Marx regarded this book as one of Engels's greatest contributions, citing it more than any other of his friend's writings in *Capital*.

Marx himself took up the Irish potato famine of the 1840s as a tragedy rooted in the process of capital accumulation, especially in *Capital*. He wrote as well about Irish workers in Britain, especially in 1869–70, at a time when the First International was substantially engaged with supporting Irish revolutionaries. While he was able to convince the International to support the Irish, it was a difficult battle. At the same time, this was a battle that needed to be fought and won, because it got to the heart of why, despite its large-scale industrialisation and organised working class, Britain had not seen the level of class struggle predicted in texts written at an abstract level like the *Communist Manifesto*. He offered an explanation in a "Confidential Communication" of the International issued in early 1870:

> [T]he English bourgeoisie has not only exploited Irish poverty to keep down the working class in England by forced immigration of poor Irishmen, but it has also divided the proletariat into two hostile camps ... The common English worker hates the Irish worker as a competitor who lowers wages and the standard of life. He feels national and religious antipathies for him. He views him similarly to how the poor whites of the Southern states of North America viewed black slaves. This antagonism among the proletarians of England is

artificially nourished and kept up by the bourgeoisie. It knows that this split is the true secret of the preservation of its power.[18]

Marx also saw this antagonism based upon the double oppression of the Irish workers, as both proletarians and as members of an oppressed minority in dialectical terms. He viewed the Irish as sources of revolutionary ferment that could help spark a British revolution. Thus, we have here the analysis of a really existing working class at a specific point in time, Britain in 1870, as opposed to the more general and abstract manner in which he and Engels conceptualised the working class in the *Manifesto*.

Marx viewed the racially divided working class of the United States (US) in similar terms. He strongly opposed slavery and advocated abolitionism within the working-class movement, attacking those like Pierre Joseph Proudhon who were more ambiguous on the subject of slavery.

He conceptualised African slavery as central to capitalist development, writing as early as *Poverty of Philosophy* (1847):

Direct slavery is just as much the pivot of bourgeois industry as machinery, credits, etc. Without slavery you have no cotton; without cotton you have no modern industry. It is slavery that gave the colonies their value; it is the colonies that created world trade, and it is world trade that is the precondition of large-scale industry.[19]

During the 1861–65 Civil War in the US, Marx strongly, albeit critically, supported the North against the slave South. He regarded the

MECW 21: 120, emphasis in original
MECW 6: 167

war as a second American revolution that had created some real possibilities for the working class. He intoned in *Capital*:

> *In the US, every independent workers' movement was paralysed as long as slavery disfigured a part of the republic. Labor in a white skin cannot emancipate itself where it is branded in a black skin. However, a new life immediately arose from the death of slavery. The first fruit of the American Civil War was the eight hours agitation, which ran from the Atlantic to the Pacific, from New England to California, with the seven-league boots of a locomotive.*[20]

At this point, he noted that a large national labour congress took place in 1866, one year after the end of the Civil War, where the demand for the eight-hour day was put forward.

Here, the abolition of slavery is seen as the precondition for a real working-class movement in the racialised capitalism of the US.

If Marx's working class was not exclusively white, nor was it exclusively male. In her study of Marx and gender, Heather Brown concludes that in the parts of *Capital* devoted to the life experience of the workers, "Marx not only traces out the changing conditions of the male worker, but also gives significant emphasis to the role of women in this process." While he sometimes lapsed into "echoing paternalistic or patriarchal assumptions" in his descriptions of female workers, it is hard to argue, as some have, that he ignored working women in his most important book.[21]

This can also be seen in his dialectical discussion of changes to the family and gender relations brought about by capitalist industrialisation, which has "dissolved the old family relationships"

20. Marx 1976: 414, emphasis added
21. Brown 2012: 91

among the workers, as women and children were forced into horribly exploitative paid employment outside the home:

However terrible and disgusting the dissolution of the old family ties within the capitalist system may appear, large-scale industry, by assigning an important part in socially organised processes of production, outside the sphere of the domestic economy, to women, young persons, and children of both sexes, does nevertheless create a new economic foundation for a higher form of the family and of relations between the sexes.[22]

Marx returned to gender and the family as a research topic at the end of his life, as seen in his *Ethnological Notebooks* of 1880–82[23] and other notebooks from that period. In these notebooks, he explored gender relations across a number of societies, from preliterate Native Americans and Homeric Greeks, to precolonial Ireland and contemporary Australian aborigines. Some of these notes became the basis for Engels's *Origin of the Family*. Although that work contains many important insights, it treats the rise of gender oppression in an economic and class reductionist manner that was far less subtle than the notes Marx left behind and which Engels used as source material.[24] These notebooks are also concerned deeply with colonialism, an issue discussed below with which Engels did not engage.

REVOLUTIONARY SUBJECTIVITY OUTSIDE THE WORKING CLASS

It is important to note that Marx's interest in gender issues was not

22. Marx 1976: 620–21
23. Krader 1974
24. Dunayevskaya 1982; Anderson 2014; Brown 2012

limited to the study of working class women. From his earliest writings, he pointed to gender oppression as a crucial, foundational form of social hierarchy and domination. In the 1844 *Manuscripts*, he wrote:

> The direct, natural, necessary relationship of human being [Mensch] to human being is the relationship of man [Mann] to woman [Weib]. ... Therefore, on the basis of this relationship, we can judge the whole stage of development of the human being. From the character of this relationship it follows to what degree the human being has become and recognised himself or herself as a species being; a human being; the relationship of man to woman is the most natural relationship of human being to human being. Therefore, in it is revealed the degree to which the natural behaviour of the human being has become human.[25]

Here, Marx is concerned not only with working-class women, as discussed above, but with other strata of women as well, and across the full trajectory of human society and culture, not just capitalism. He takes up the oppression of modern women outside the working class in his 1846 text, "Peuchet on Suicide," where he focuses on middle- and upper-class French women driven to suicide by gender-based oppression from husbands or parents, writing at one point of "social conditions ... which permit the jealous husband to fetter his wife in chains, like a miser with his hoard of gold, for she is but part of his inventory."[26] These concerns did not end with Marx's youth. In 1858, he wrote movingly in the *New York Tribune*

25. Quoted in Plaut and Anderson 1999: 6, emphasis in original; see also MECW 3: 295–96 for an earlier translation)
26. Plaut and Anderson 1999: 58

about Lady Rosina Bulwer Lytton, who had been confined to a mental institution by her politician husband for having attempted to speak out on political issues.[27]

Nor did Marx focus on the industrial working class to the exclusion of the peasantry, which he saw as an oppressed and potentially revolutionary class. Considerable attention has been paid to his characterisation of the French peasantry as somewhat conservative in the *Eighteenth Brumaire of Louis Bonaparte* (1852). In other contexts, though, he discussed the revolutionary potential of peasants, for example, during the 16th-century Anabaptist uprising in Germany. Concerning his own time, in the *Critique of the Gotha Programme* (1875), he castigated Ferdinand Lassalle for labelling the "peasants" as inherently conservative, since Lassalle's organisation had written off "all other classes" besides the working class as "one reactionary mass".[28]

And, while condemning racist and imperialist forms of nationalism, Marx also strongly supported nationalist movements that exhibited a clear emancipatory content. Long before Vladimir Ilich Lenin articulated a concept of national liberation, in an 1848 speech on Poland, Marx drew a distinction between what he termed "narrowly national [*étroitement national*]" movements and national revolutions that were "reforming and democratic," that is, ones that put forth issues like land reform even when it targeted the indigenous upper classes rather than just a foreign enemy or occupying power.[29]

Even in the *Communist Manifesto*, where, as discussed above, he and Engels had written that national differences were disappear-

Dunayevskaya 1982; Brown 2012
MECW 24: 88–89
Marx 1994: 1001, my translation from the French original; see also MECW 6: 549

ing, this was at a general, abstract level. For, when it came down to concretising the principles in terms of a set of immediate goals and slogans in a final section, "Position of the Communists in Relation to the Existing Opposition Parties," Polish national emancipation from under Russian, Austrian, and Prussian occupation was nonetheless singled out: "In Poland, they support the party that insists on an agrarian revolution as the prime condition for national emancipation, that party which fomented the insurrection of Cracow in 1846".[30] Marx continued to support a Polish national revolution until the end of his life. He greeted the Polish uprising of 1863 with enthusiasm and in his writings celebrating the Paris Commune of 1871; he singled out the important contribution of Polish exiles in the military defence of revolutionary Paris. Fittingly, in Père Lachaise cemetery in Paris, the graves of the Communards include that of Polish General Walery Wróblewski, only steps away from those of Marx's French descendants.

In the 1870 *Confidential Communication on Ireland*, the peasantry and the national movement were also intertwined as revolutionary elements. An equally prominent point in this text is Marx's defence of the International's public support of Irish national emancipation, including appeals to the Queen to stop the execution of Irish militants. On this issue, Marx and the International's General Council in London had come under attack by the anarchist Mikhail Bakunin's faction, which took a class-reductionist position, rejecting "any political action that does not have as its immediate and direct aim the triumph of the workers' cause against capital".[31] In response, Marx wrote in the *Communication*:

---

30. MECW 6: 518
31. Quoted in MECW 21: 208

In the first place, Ireland is the bulwark of English landlordism. If it fell in Ireland, it would fall in England. In Ireland this is a hundred times easier because the economic struggle there is concentrated exclusively on landed property, because this struggle is at the same time national, and because the people there are more revolutionary and angrier than in England. Landlordism in Ireland is maintained solely by the English army. The moment the forced Union between the two countries ends, a social revolution will immediately break out in Ireland.[32]

Moreover, he hinted that such a process could also break the impasse in which British workers were stuck:

Although revolutionary initiative will probably come from France, England alone can serve as the lever for a serious economic Revolution ... It is the only country where the vast majority of the population consists of wage laborers ... The English have all the material conditions [matière nécessaire] for social revolution. What they lack is a sense of generalisation and revolutionary passion. It is only the General Council that can provide them with this, that can thus accelerate the truly revolutionary movement in this country, and consequently everywhere ... If England is the bulwark of landlordism and European capitalism, the only point where official England can be struck a great blow is Ireland.[33]

MECW 21: 119–120, translation slightly altered on basis of French original in Marx 1966: 358–59

MECW 21: 118–19, translation slightly altered on basis of French original in Marx 1966: 356–57

He conceptualised more explicitly this notion of the Irish struggle for independence as a detonator for a wider British and European working-class revolution in a letter to Engels of 10 December 1869:

> *For a long time I believed that it would be possible to overthrow the Irish regime by English working-class ascendancy. I always expressed this point of view in the New York Tribune. Deeper study has now convinced me of the opposite. The English working class will never accomplish anything before it has got rid of Ireland. The lever must be applied in Ireland. That is why the Irish question is so important for the social movement in general.*[34]

Here, Marx also acknowledges explicitly a change of position, from an earlier one, where he saw proletarian revolution spreading from the core industrial nations to the periphery. At this point, he is beginning to develop the notion of a transnational communist revolution beginning in the more agrarian, colonised peripheries of capitalism, and then spreading into the core nations. During the last years before his death in 1883, this was to become a major concern with respect to societies outside Western Europe and North America.

Late Marx: India, Russia, and Beyond

In *The German Ideology* of 1846, Marx and Engels conceptualised several successive stages of historical development in Eurocentric terms, later called modes of production: (i) clan or tribal, (ii) slave-based ancient Greco–Roman, (iii) serf-based feudal, (iv) formally

---

34. MECW 43: 398, emphasis in original

free wage-labour-based bourgeois or capitalist, and, it was implied, (v) freely-associated-labour-based socialist. A decade later, in the *Grundrisse* of 1857–58, Marx discussed modes of production originating in Asia, especially India (the "Asiatic" mode of production) as a type of pre-capitalist system that did not fall easily under either (ii) or (iii). It represented something qualitatively different, without as much formal slavery, and with communal or collective property and social relations continuing in the villages for a very long time.

For Marx, this constituted a more global and multilinear theory of history, with premodern Asian societies on a somewhat different pathway of development than Western Europe, especially ancient Rome. In *Capital*, Vol I, he referred to "the ancient Asiatic, Classical-antique, and other such modes of production," where commodity production "plays a subordinate role" as compared to the modern capitalist mode of production.[35] Marx's distinction between Asian and European pre-capitalist societies was banned in Stalinist ideology, which clung to the slavery–feudal–bourgeois model of successive modes of production, something that required mental gymnastics to fit societies like Mughal India or Confucian China into the "feudal" or "slave" modes of production. Even as late as the 1970s, the noted anthropologist and Marx scholar Norair Ter-Akopian was dismissed from the Marx–Engels–Lenin Institute in Moscow for having published a book on the Asiatic mode of production.

In notes from his last years not published until after Stalin's death, Marx summarised and commented upon his young anthropologist friend Maxim Kovalevsky's *Communal Property* (1879), especially its treatment of precolonial India. Although appreciative of much of Kovalevsky's analysis, Marx inveighed against his attempts to treat Mughal India, with its highly centralised state system, as feudal: "Kovalevsky here finds feudalism in the Western European sense. Kovalevsky forgets, among other things, serfdom, which is not in India, and which is an essential moment." Marx concludes that concerning "feudalism," "as little is found in India as in Rome".[36] These notes, available in English since 1975, did not find their way into the *Collected Works* of Marx and Engels. Nor can any of the notes on Kovalevsky or other late texts on India be found in the most recent collection of Marx's India writings.[37] However, Irfan Habib's comprehensive introduction to this volume does mention briefly the late Marx's notebooks on India his "objection to any designation of the Indian communities as 'feudal'."[38]

All this would be only an academic topic had Marx not tied these issues to the contemporary issues of colonialism and world revolution. In the years 1848–53, Marx tended toward an implicit support of colonialism, whether in forcing a traditionalist China into the world market, as quoted above from the *Communist Manifesto*, or in his 1853 articles on India, which celebrated what he saw as modernising and progressive aspects of British rule. In 1853, he portrays India as backward in socio-economic terms, incapable of real change from within, and unable to mount serious resistance to foreign invasion due to its social divisions. Therefore, he could write that year in his *Tribune* article, "British Rule in India," that British colonialism was carrying in its wake "the greatest, and to speak

---

36. Krader 1975: 383
37. Husain 2006
38. Husain 2006: xxxv

the truth, the only social revolution ever heard of in Asia."[39]To be sure, Edward Said and others have caricatured his 1853 India articles as completely pro-colonialist, ignoring another major one a few weeks later, "The Future Results of British Rule in India," which attacks the "barbarism" of British colonialism and applauds the possibility of India being able one day "to throw off the English yoke altogether".[40] Nonetheless, some of Said's criticisms are on target with regard to the Eurocentrism and ethnocentrism of the 1853 writings.

By the time of the *Grundrisse* of 1857–58, with its discussion of precolonial India being on a different historical trajectory than ancient Rome, Marx was also coming out publicly, again in the *Tribune*, in support of both the anti-British sepoy uprising in India and Chinese resistance to the British in the Second Opium War. But, his support for this anti-colonial resistance remained at a rather general level. Marx did not embrace the overall political aims or perspectives of the Chinese or Indians resisting imperialism, which seemed to be neither democratic nor communist.[41] This differs from his late writings on Russia, which saw emancipatory communist movements emerging from that country's communal villages. Thus, Marx's thinking on these issues seems to have evolved further after 1858.

MULTILINEAR PATHWAYS OF DEVELOPMENT AND REVOLUTION

During his last years, Marx never finished Volumes 2 and 3 of *Cap-*

MECW 12: 132
(MECW 12: 221).
Benner 2018

ital, although he reworked Vol I painstakingly for the French edition of 1872–75, altering several passages that were seen to imply that societies outside the narrow band of industrialising capitalism would inevitably have to modernise in the Western industrial sense. In the original 1867 edition, he had written: "The country that is more developed industrially only shows, to the less developed, the image of its own future".[42] Even the usually careful scholar Teodor Shanin viewed this passage as an example of "unilinear determinism".[43] He, therefore, drew a sharp distinction between *Capital* (determinist) and Marx's late writings on Russia (open-ended and multilinear). But, Shanin and other scholars who taxed Marx for this passage did not notice that in the subsequent 1872–75 French edition, the last version of the book he himself saw to publication, he recast this passage: "The country that is more developed industrially only shows, to those that follow it up the industrial ladder [*le suivent sur l'échelle industrielle*], the image of its own future."[44] In this way, he removed any hint of unilinear determinism and, more importantly, suggested that the future of societies outside Western Europe might follow a different pathway.

Marx made a much more explicit statement concerning his multilinear approach to the historical possibilities of agrarian societies outside Western Europe in the draft of an 1877 letter, where he criticised strongly any idea of "transforming my historical sketch [in the "Primitive Accumulation" section of *Capital*—KA] of the genesis of capitalism in Western Europe into a historico-philosophical theory of the general course fatally imposed on all peoples, whatever the historical circumstances in which they find themselves

42. Marx 1976: 91
43. Shanin 1983: 4
44. Marx 1976: 91, my translation, see also Anderson 2014

22

placed," a letter in which he also quoted the French edition of *Capital*.[45]

Marx also returned at length to the subject of India in his above-cited 1879 notes on Kovalevsky[46], his *Notes on Indian History*[47], and his 1880–82 *Ethnological Notebooks*.[48] During these last years, he wrote of Russian peasant "primitive communism" as a locus of resistance to capital and of possible linkages to the revolutionary working-class communist movement in the West. This is seen in a famous passage from his last published text, the 1882 preface he and Engels contributed to a new Russian edition of the *Communist Manifesto*:

If the Russian revolution becomes the signal for a proletarian revolution in the West, so that the two complement each other, then the present Russian common ownership [*Gemeineigentum*] may serve as the point of departure [*Ausgungspunkt*] for a communist development.[49]

In his late writings on Russia and notebooks on South Asia, North Africa, Latin America, and a number of other agrarian, pastoral, or hunter-gatherer societies, Marx is deeply concerned with the rise of gender and social hierarchy during the decline of communal social formations.[50] It is also very likely that he was interested in South Asian, North African, Latin American villages, like

---

Shanin 1983: 136.

. Krader 1975

. Marx 1960

. Krader 1974

Shanin 1983: 139, see also MECW 24: 426 and MEW 19: 296, translation slightly altered

Some of these notebooks are still unpublished and will appear in the *Marx–Engels Gesamtausgabe* or MEGA, but their aspects have been discussed in Brown 2012; Pradella 2015 and Anderson 2016.

the Russian ones, as possible loci of resistance to capital and there-fore potential allies of the working classes of Western Europe and North America.

For example, in Marx's notes on Kovalevsky's lengthy discussion of India, he traces in great detail the shift from kin-based com-munal village organisation to one grounded more in mere resi-dency. At this stage, he has clearly rejected his earlier notion of an unchanging India until the arrival of capitalism via the British. However, as against his writings on Ireland, he never acknowledges this change explicitly, as in his 1869 letter to Engels on Ireland cited above. (Of course, we have less information on Marx's thinking in his last years. By 1879, Engels, his most regular intellectual inter-locutor, was no longer in faraway Manchester receiving Marx's letters, but a neighbour who visited almost daily but without leav-ing much of paper trail of their conversations. Marx's letters to Kovalevsky were also burned by his friends in Russia, who went to his house to do so, out of fear of them falling into the hands the police, which could have endangered the young anthropologist.)

As seen above, as early as the 1857 sepoy uprising, Marx seems to have moved away from his earlier notion of India as a passive civil-isation that did not offer much resistance to foreign conquest. He recorded detailed data on Indian resistance in another set of notes taken around 1879, on British colonial official Robert Sewell's *Ana-lytical History of India* (1870), published in Moscow as Marx's *Notes on Indian History*[51] without awareness that this volume consisted mainly of passages excerpted from Sewell's book. In these notes, Marx records dozens of examples of Indian resistance to foreign invaders and domestic rulers, from the earliest historical records

51. Marx 1960

right up through the sepoy uprising. Moreover, Marx's notes now view Mughal, British, and other conquests of India as contingent rather than the product of ineluctable social forces.

But, Marx's main focus in these late notebooks on South Asia, North Africa, and Latin America is the structure and history of communal social relations and property in these regions, and on how colonialism uprooted these earlier social relations. At the same time, as a dialectical thinker, Marx also notes the persistence of remnants of these communal social forms even after they had been greatly undermined by colonialism. Did he come to believe that the Indian, Algerian, or Latin American village could become a locus of resistance to capital, as he had theorised in 1882 concerning the Russian village? That is what I have concluded after years of study of these notebooks.

To be sure, he never said such a thing explicitly. Moreover, in his late writings on Russia, in the drafts of his 1881 letter to Vera Zasulich, he even noted a key difference with India, that Russia had not "fallen prey, like the East Indies, to a conquering foreign power". [52]

Still, I find it hard to believe that Marx engaged in such a deep and extended study of the communal social formations in pre-colonial and even colonial South Asia, North Africa, and Latin America without an aim beyond purely historical research. As the Italian Marx scholar Luca Basso notes, Marx was in his late writings on Russia and other non-Western societies, operating on "two planes," that of "historical-theoretical interpretation" and that of "the feasibility or otherwise of a revolutionary movement" in the

2. Shanin 1983: 106

context of what he was studying.[53] The fact that he undertook this research in the years just before his clarion call in the 1882 preface to the *Manifesto* about an uprising in Russia's communal villages that would link up with the Western proletariat as the "starting point for a communist revolution" suggests the connectedness of all of this research on primitive communism. As Dunayevskaya argued in the first work that linked these notebooks to modern concerns with revolution and women's liberation: "Marx returns to probe the origin of humanity, not for purposes of discovering new origins, but for perceiving new revolutionary forces, their reason."[54]

It is important to see both his brilliant generalisations about capitalist society and the very concrete ways in which he examined not only class, but also gender, race, and colonialism, and what today would be called the intersectionality of all of these. His underlying revolutionary humanism was the enemy of all forms of abstraction that denied the variety and multiplicity of human experience, especially as his vision extended outward from Western Europe. For these reasons, no thinker speaks to us today with such force and clarity.

53. Basso 2015: 90
54. Dunayevskaya 1982: 187

BIBLIOGRAPHY

Anderson, Kevin B (2014): *Marx at the Margins: On Nationalism, Ethnicity, and Non-Western Societies*, New Delhi: Pinnacle Learning.

— (2016): *Marx at the Margins: On Nationalism, Ethnicity, and Non-Western Societies*, Expanded edition, Chicago: University of Chicago Press.

Basso, Luca (2015): *Marx and the Common: From Capital to the Late Writings*, Trans David Broder, Leiden: Brill.

Benner, Erica (2018): *Really Existing Nationalisms: A Post-Communist View from Marx and Engels*, Reprint edition, New York: Oxford University Press.

Brown, Heather (2012): *Marx on Gender and the Family*, Leiden: Brill.

Chattopadhyay, Paresh (2016): *Marx's Associated Mode of Production*, New York: Palgrave.

Dunayevskaya, Raya (1958): *Marxism and Freedom*, New York: Bookman Associates.

— (1982): *Rosa Luxemburg, Women's Liberation, and Marx's Philosophy of Revolution*, Sussex: Harvester Press.

Hegel, G W F (2018): *Phenomenology of Spirit*, Trans Michael Inwood, New York: Oxford University Press.

Hudis, Peter (2012): *Marx's Concept of the Alternative to Capitalism*, Leiden: Brill.

Husain, Iqbal (ed) (2006): *Karl Marx on India*, New Delhi: Tulika Books.

27

Kosík, Karel (1976): *Dialectics of the Concrete*, Trans Karel Kovanda and James Schmidt, Boston: D Reidel.

Krader, Lawrence (ed) (1974): *The Ethnological Notebooks of Karl Marx*, Second Edition, Assen: Van Gorcum.

— (1975): *The Asiatic Mode of Production*, Assen: Van Gorcum.

Marx, Karl (1960): *Notes on Indian History (664–1858)*, Moscow: Progress Publishers.

— (1966): "Le conseil générale au conseil fédérale de la Suisse romande," *General Council of the First International 1868–1870, Minutes*, Moscow: Progress Publishers.

— (1976): *Capital: A Critique of Political Economy*, Vol 1, Trans Ben Fowkes, New York: Penguin.

— (1994): *Oeuvres* IV, Edited by Maximilien Rubel, Paris: Éditions Gallimard.

[MECW] Marx, Karl and Frederick Engels (1975–2004): *Collected Works*, Fifty Volumes, New York: International Publishers.

[MEW] Marx, Karl and Friedrich Engels (1968): *Werke*, Berlin: Dietz Verlag.

Ollman, Bertell (1993): *Dialectical Investigations*, New York: Routledge.

Plaut, Eric A and Kevin B Anderson (1999): *Marx on Suicide*, Evanston: Northwestern University Press.

Pradella, Lucia (2015): *Globalisation and the Critique of Political Economy: New Insights from Marx's Writings*, Milton Park: Routledge.

Shanin, Teodor (1983): *Late Marx and the Russian Road*, New York: Monthly Review Press.

Lightning Source UK Ltd.
Milton Keynes UK
UKHW022044130920
369846UK00006B/277